Walter Tull:
Footballer, Soldier, Hero

Contents

Written by Dan Lyndon

Illustrated by Roger Wade Walker

Reporting for duty

"Officer Tull, reporting for duty, Sir!"

"Very good, Tull. Stand at ease. Now listen here, this is your first mission and it's not an easy one, I'm afraid. We need you to take your men across to Hill 67 and capture it from the Germans. I've been very impressed with what I've heard about you. Your King and country are relying on you, don't let them down. That's all."

"Thank you, General."

After his briefing with the General, Walter lay back on his bunk and thought about how far he'd come from the children's home in east London where he'd grown up after his parents had died. At 28 years old, Walter was the first black soldier to become an **Infantry Officer** in the British Army and had been one of the first black professional footballers in Britain. He'd travelled to faraway places like Argentina and Italy and now he was fighting in France. If only his family could see him now …

Grandma Tull

Walter Tull's grandmother, Anna, had been born a **slave** in Barbados, a small island in the Caribbean. The first slaves had arrived in Barbados at the end of the 17th century when the British ruled the island. They came from different parts of West Africa, where many had been captured as prisoners of war or kidnapped and later sold by people called slave traders.

Walter's grandmother, Anna

The Africans were forced on to the slave ships and sailed across the Atlantic Ocean to the Caribbean or the USA. The slave ships were very overcrowded, with men, women and children kept below the deck. There were no toilets and disease spread easily. Often the men were chained together to prevent them from resisting. Anyone who tried to escape was whipped.

Over ten million Africans were enslaved between 1450 and 1833 and as many as two million died on the journey across the Atlantic. When they arrived, the Africans that had survived were sold into slavery at **auctions**.

Life as a slave was incredibly hard. Africans were made to work from daylight to dusk on the plantations, which were large farms, doing back-breaking work like cutting sugar cane and growing tobacco. There was an overseer who was paid to make sure the slaves worked as hard as possible. If they didn't do their work or they were tired, the overseer would whip them.

Although the slaves weren't paid for their work, they had their clothes and housing provided for them. However, many of the slaves lived in terrible conditions, in very basic and run-down buildings. They slept on straw and sometimes the farm animals lived in the same room.

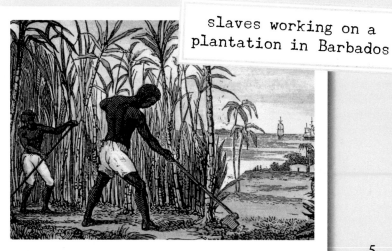

slaves working on a plantation in Barbados

Daniel Tull

After the **abolition** of slavery in the Caribbean in 1833,
many freed slaves were paid to carry on working on
the plantations, but some of them took apprenticeships.
This meant that they learnt a trade from a skilled person,
such as a carpenter, who worked with wood.

Daniel Tull, Walter Tull's grandfather, was born after
the abolition of slavery. He went to school with his brothers
and sisters, next to the chapel at Clifton Hill. When he left
school, Daniel Tull started work as an apprentice carpenter
in Barbados, earning sixpence a week.

This wasn't a very good wage and it was a struggle to be able to afford enough food for the week, when a loaf of bread and some milk could cost a penny each. Sometimes Daniel didn't get paid at all because his master didn't have enough money to pay his apprentices. However, when he went to complain, he was given a beating. Daniel decided to leave Barbados and try to find some work on one of the other islands.

The boat from the Caribbean

In the 19th century, many of the Caribbean Islands were part of the **British Empire**, which was ruled by Queen Victoria. Daniel Tull's friends said that there were lots of jobs in England and carpenters could earn five shillings a day. That was much more than he was earning in Barbados. In the summer of 1876, when Daniel heard that a ship sailing to England needed a carpenter on board, he jumped at the chance and joined the crew.

The journey from the Caribbean to London took about six weeks on board a sailing ship, depending on the strength of the winds. It wasn't until the 1880s that steamships, which carried about 400 passengers, regularly crossed the Atlantic in much faster times. The conditions on board the sailing ships were very cramped, especially if the weather was bad and the passengers had to go below deck. Passengers also had to bring their own food to eat.

Caribbean Sea

This was usually salted fish or dried meat. Food that had been preserved in salt or dried out lasted for months. Some passengers even brought barrels of beer for the journey. As the ship's carpenter, Daniel Tull had to make repairs to any of the timber that got damaged and he was responsible for the ship's anchor. When the ship docked in Folkestone on the south-east coast of England, Daniel decided to stay there and try to find work.

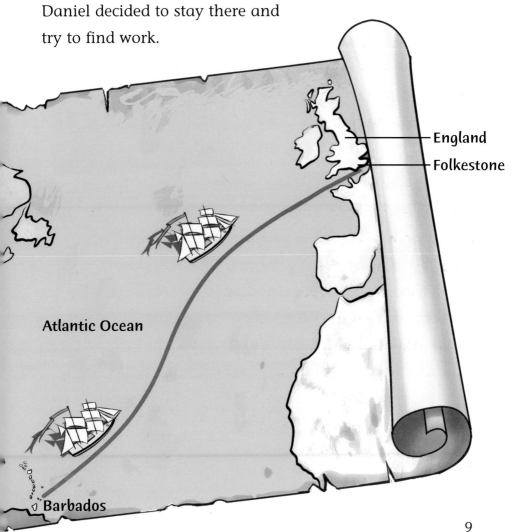

England

Folkestone

Atlantic Ocean

Barbados

The Palmers

Walter Tull's mother,
Alice Palmer, grew up in
Folkestone. She came from
a poor family, most of whom
worked on the land for the
local farmers, which is where
many people who could not
afford to go to school were
employed. Their jobs included
ploughing land, sowing seeds
and harvesting the crops.

There weren't many black people living in Folkestone at
that time, but as Daniel had a trade and he had taught
himself to read and write, he was able to find work
regularly and as a result was able to pay for a room in
the town. Just as he'd done in Barbados, Daniel also went
to the Methodist Chapel on Sundays, which is where
he met Alice.

In 1881 Alice and Daniel got married. There weren't
many mixed-race marriages at the time, but as there were
more black men than black women living in England,
most of them married white women.

Both Daniel and Alice came from working-class backgrounds so there was less reaction to their marriage than if they'd come from the middle or upper classes. Alice's family were very happy to have Daniel as their new son-in-law and Alice's mother wrote to Daniel welcoming him.

farmland in the 1880s

Walton Road

Daniel and Alice had six children: Bertha, William, Cecillia, Edward, Walter and Elsie. They all lived at 51 Walton Road in Folkestone. It was very crowded in their house, so the boys shared one bed and the girls shared another. Walter and his brothers attended the North Board Elementary School.

North Board Elementary School

Moving on

When Walter was five years old his mother died, having been ill for a long time with cancer.

Life was hard for Daniel, who had to look after his six children, all under the age of 14, on his own and earn a living. So Clara, Alice's niece, came to help. Daniel and Clara fell in love and got married on 17 October 1896.

Then, on 10 December 1897, just two years after Alice had died, Daniel died from heart disease and Clara was left on her own looking after what was now a family of seven children.
Clara didn't have much money and her family were poor and couldn't support her, so Walter and Edward were sent to a children's home in east London. Walter was eight years old.

Cecillia, William, Walter, Edward, Daniel (father), Elsie (on Daniel's lap)

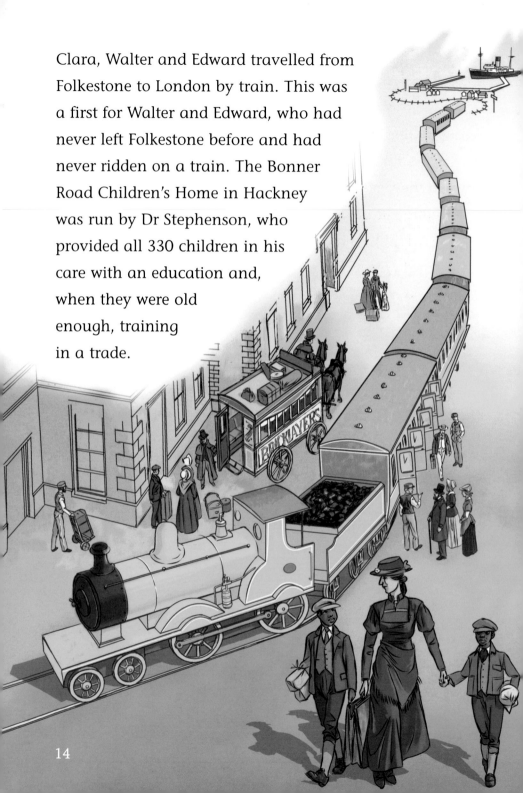

Clara, Walter and Edward travelled from Folkestone to London by train. This was a first for Walter and Edward, who had never left Folkestone before and had never ridden on a train. The Bonner Road Children's Home in Hackney was run by Dr Stephenson, who provided all 330 children in his care with an education and, when they were old enough, training in a trade.

14

The children's home

The children's home was organised like a big family home. The children went to school during the day and when they'd finished their evening meal they had two hours of free time before "lights out" at 8 o'clock. Walter was very athletic and, although he excelled at cricket, he spent his free time playing football for the home's team, becoming its star player.

Walter and Edward were happy at the Bonner Road Children's Home, but on 14 November 1900, when Walter was ten years old, nearly three years after arriving, the brothers were separated when Edward was adopted by a family in Glasgow. Edward left the children's home and Walter, but the family remained united and Walter visited him in Glasgow.

Bonner Road Children's Home

THE CHILDRENS HOME

Clever footwork

By the time he was 16, Walter had been playing left-wing and left-back for the orphanage football team for a few years. He'd become very good and was invited to go for a trial at a local **amateur** team called Clapton. The trial went very well and Walter was asked to join the team. Walter was the first black footballer to play for Clapton and he performed so well that *The Football Star* newspaper praised his "clever footwork" on the pitch.

Footballers had to be strong and fit because the game was much more physical then – tackles were harder and the goalkeeper could be knocked into the back of the net. Even the ball was really hard, because it was made from heavy leather, unlike the lightweight balls used today. If a ball wasn't headed properly players could knock themselves out! Although Walter wasn't very tall, playing football made him a strong young man.

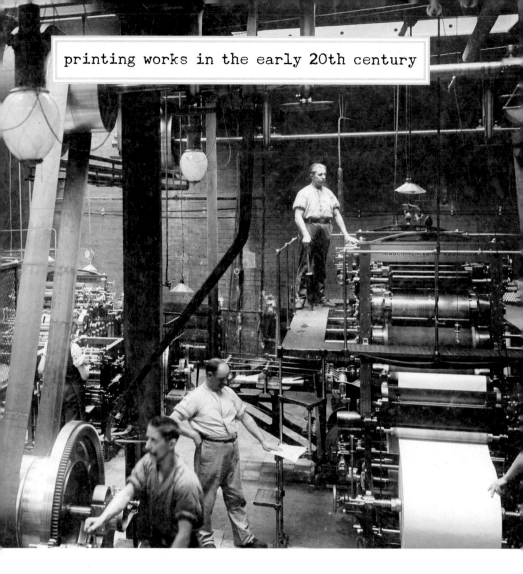

Because amateur footballers didn't make any money,
Walter decided to train as a printer in the workshops at
the children's home at the same time as playing for Clapton.
Walter dreamt of becoming a professional football player,
but he knew that if he wasn't good enough, he could use
his training as a printer to earn a living.

18

The 1908 season

Walter was playing regularly for Clapton. As centre-forward, the position he played on the pitch, Walter scored plenty of goals and the team was on the up. The first final that Walter played in was the FA Amateur Challenge Cup, against a team from the Northern League, Eston United. Clapton won 6–0, which was a record result in that competition. Walter had been with Clapton only two years and the club was on its way to being one of the top amateur teams in the country.

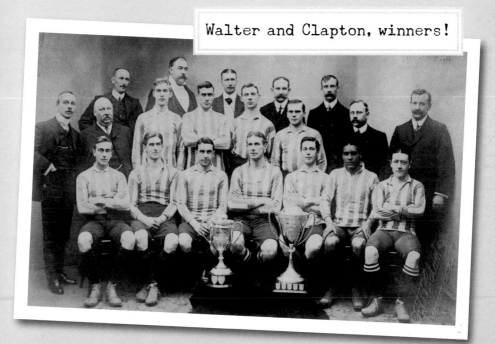

Walter and Clapton, winners!

Going pro

Clapton reached the London Senior Cup final and then the London County Amateur Cup final. Walter was described in *The Football Star* as "Clapton's catch of the season" and talent scouts from professional teams came to watch him play. Tottenham Hotspur, then the richest team in London, invited Walter for a trial and he played in their reserve team, scoring twice in a friendly against Clapton Orient. This was enough to impress the manager at Tottenham Hotspur, who offered Walter a **contract**. As he'd finished his apprenticeship as a printer, he was free to play football professionally. Walter earned a £10 signing-on fee and was paid £4 a week, the maximum wage for a footballer at that time.

Tottenham Hotspur football ground in 1910

TOTTENHAM HOTSPUR
FOOTBALL CLUB

Tottenham Hotspur was in the **First Division**, and crowds of over 15,000 people watched the team's games – more than five times bigger than the crowds Clapton played in front of at the Old Spotted Dog ground in Upton Lane. Walter was the first black footballer to play for Tottenham and only the third black man to play professional football in the UK.

He followed in the footsteps of Andrew Watson, who played for Queen's Park in 1875, and Arthur Wharton, goalkeeper for Rotherham United in 1889 and for Sheffield United in 1894.

Walter in his
Tottenham Hotspur kit

21

On tour

At the end of the season Walter was invited to join
Tottenham's tour of Argentina and Uruguay. Andrew Watson
had been the first black South American to play in Britain,
but Walter was the first black British footballer to play in
South America. The longest trip Walter had ever taken
was from Folkestone to London and he'd never been on
a boat. Now he was travelling halfway round the world.
The team set sail for South America in May 1909, on
the journey across the Atlantic that Walter's father Daniel
had made in the opposite direction 33 years earlier.

It took weeks to sail from England to South America. The team kept fit on the long journey by running around the deck of the ship. Playing in South America was tough because it was so hot and Walter wrote home to his friends saying that he thought he'd got sunstroke.

Walter had great success on the tour, playing centre-forward for Tottenham and scoring against Everton in a 2–2 draw. He even got a mention in the *Buenos Aires Herald*, which said that he was a favourite with the local crowd.
He'd come a long way from playing for the children's home team in east London.

Tough times

Back home, Walter was soon making an impact at Tottenham Hotspur, winning a penalty against Manchester United and scoring his first goal against Bradford City two weeks after making his **debut** in the **league**. But it wasn't long afterwards that his experience at Tottenham turned sour.

Walter was chosen to play against Bristol City at their ground, Ashton Gate, in front of a crowd of nearly 20,000 people. Although he wasn't the first black professional footballer, Walter was the only black player in the league at that time. Up until this point Walter hadn't experienced anything to suggest that the colour of his skin would have affected his football career.

Early in the second half of the game, Walter was involved in an incident on the pitch with one of the Bristol players. When the referee waved for play to go on, the Bristol supporters in the crowd were so angry that some of them shouted abuse and made **racist** comments about Walter.

Although he continued to play until the end of the game, and was described by one journalist as "the best forward on the field" and in "a class superior to that shown by most of his colleagues", the directors at Tottenham Hotspur retired Walter from the first team to stop more racist abuse in future games. He was only chosen to play for the team three more times.

The Cobblers

Herbert Chapman, the manager of Second Division team
Northampton Town (known as "The Cobblers" because
lots of shoes were made in Northampton), was looking
for a new left-footed centre-forward to join his team.
He'd heard that there was a skilful player in the reserves
at Tottenham Hotspur who might be able to do the job
for him. Walter was transferred to Northampton in
October 1911 and it was reported in the newspapers
that Chapman paid "a heavy transfer fee" for him.

Northampton was very different from the East End of London – there were fewer dirty, smelly factories and more green fields. Walter moved to a small town nearby called Rushden, where he rented a room. Footballers earned a good wage, but this was still not enough for them to be able to afford to buy their own houses, unlike multimillionaire footballers today. Walter was still in close contact with his brother, and Edward even travelled from Glasgow to watch him play.

the house where
Walter rented a room

Walter made his debut for Northampton Town against Watford, in front of a crowd of 5,000 people. He made his mark when he scored six goals in three games, four of them in one game against Bristol Rovers. One of the Northampton newspapers wrote that "he was a favourite with the crowd". Walter was the first black player Northampton Town had signed and even though there weren't many black people living in the area, he wasn't subjected to the kind of racial abuse he'd experienced with other football crowds.

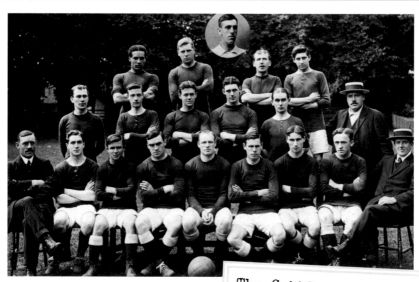

The Cobblers in 1912–13

Walter was a gifted athlete, and while he was playing
football for The Cobblers he was chosen to play cricket
for Rushden Town during the summer season.

At the end of the football season Walter was moved to
the midfield position where he linked the attack and
the defence, and he played more than 100 games for
Northampton Town. Although Walter had a successful
career, he missed his family and in 1914 made plans
to move to Glasgow Rangers, where he would be reunited
with his brother Edward. However, Walter never made it
to Glasgow.

War breaks out

Tension had been building up in Europe for many years, particularly between Britain, Germany and France. On 28 June 1914 the son of the Austrian Emperor, Archduke Franz Ferdinand, was assassinated in Sarajevo, Bosnia, in eastern Europe. Three months later, after the German Army attacked Belgium, the British Government declared war on Germany. The British Army set off for France in September 1914 to stop the German Army from attacking Paris.

war is declared, 1914

Posters asked for men to join up,
particularly fit sportsmen like Walter.
Walter was released from his contract
with Northampton football club and
on 21 December 1914 he arrived in
London to **enlist** in the Army.
Many soldiers joined "Pals' Battalions"
made up of men from the same towns,
or those who had the same job.

Walter chose to join the Footballers' Battalion
of the Middlesex Regiment for the same reason.
By 1915 the Footballers' Battalion had over a thousand
amateur and professional football players amongst its
ranks. Walter was the first footballer from Northampton
Town to join the regiment – but not the last.

Walter joins up

The Footballers' Battalion

By joining the Footballers' Battalion, where he would have been well known, Walter avoided some of the problems that other black men faced when they wanted to join the Army. In 1914 it was still rare for black people to be treated as equals with white people. The leaders of the British Army believed that black people weren't as intelligent as white people and that white soldiers would be **demoralised** if they were fighting side by side with black soldiers. Some black men who had volunteered for the Army had been turned away for failing a medical test, but it would have been difficult to fail a professional footballer on fitness grounds!

poster for the
Footballers' Battalion

Walter was sent to northern France in December 1915 with the Middlesex Regiment. He was a very good soldier and by the time he arrived in France he'd already been promoted three times. At just 26 years old, Walter was now a **Lance Sergeant**.

Life for Walter and his fellow soldiers in the trenches was tough. Trenches were very long ditches that were dug by the soldiers. They were often filled with water, so the soldiers' feet were cold and wet, and there were lots of rats spreading disease and eating the soldiers' food. There was also constant bombing by German planes and the threat of poison gas. The noise of the guns was so loud that it could be heard all the way across the Channel in England.

Walter was an experienced soldier, known for his courage and bravery. However, during May 1916 he was sent to a hospital in England to recover from shell shock, a condition caused by spending a long time in the thick of battle that would have made him feel very nervous and anxious. Some men who fought in the war never got over shell shock and spent the rest of their lives in hospital. However, after three months, Walter recovered and arrived back in France on 20 September 1916 to join up with the rest of the Middlesex Regiment. They received their orders to go to the Somme on 29 October 1916.

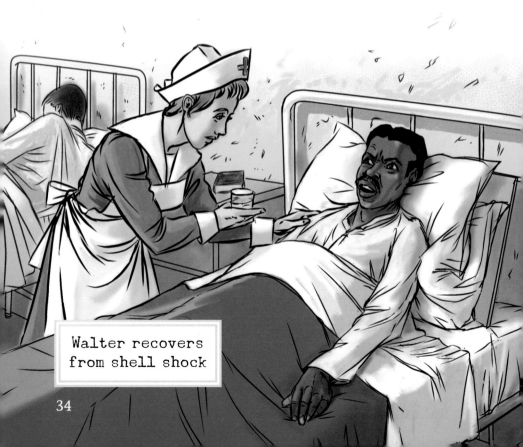

Walter recovers
from shell shock

The Battle of the Somme

On 1 July 1916 one of
the most important battles
of the First World War began
in an area of France known
as the Somme. The British
Generals who planned the
battle were confident that
they would be able to defeat
the German Army quickly
and easily, but they
were wrong.

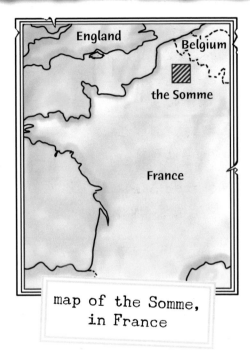

map of the Somme,
in France

The British soldiers had to walk
through an area called
No Man's Land, a strip of land
that separated the Allies from
the Germans. Walter had to dodge
machine-gun bullets and barbed
wire, deep trenches made by
exploding shells and the bodies
of soldiers who had been killed.

On the very first day of the battle there were over 50,000 British soldiers killed and wounded. After three weeks of fighting at the Somme, Walter and the rest of the Middlesex Regiment were told to move back to the rear to get a well-deserved break from the fighting.

The Battle of the Somme lasted for five months and hundreds of thousands of men on both sides were killed. By the time the battle was over in November 1916, over one and a half million men had been killed or wounded in the fighting. Of the 400 men of Walter's Middlesex Regiment who went to fight, only 79 returned.

Officer Class

Walter arrived back in England on Boxing Day 1916, the first time that he'd been given **leave** since joining the Army. Walter had been recommended by Lieutenant Colonel Haig Brown to take part in an officer training course in Scotland. There were two other black officers in the British Army, but they were in the Medical units and did not command other soldiers. Walter's inclusion on the course showed a significant change in attitude towards black people by the Army even though this was not officially recognised.

soldiers returning from the front line

During four months
of training, Walter learnt
how to train and command
groups of soldiers, how to
attack and defend against
the enemy and how to read
maps. He also learnt how
to throw grenades and build
trenches. All of these were
vital skills that soldiers
needed to use, but officers also needed to learn how
to organise and manage large groups of men and
support them in very dangerous situations.

Walter in uniform

officer training camp

The trainee officers were given manuals that covered in great detail all of the different scenarios that they would have to deal with.

This ranged from setting up a machine-gun post, to using pigeons to send secret messages.

As part of the training, every trainee would be tested to make sure that they knew everything in the manual. Walter also needed to demonstrate **initiative** and leadership and show a great deal of self-confidence. He took his exams at the end of May and graduated on 29 May 1917.

Officer Walter Tull

Walter Tull becomes an officer
in the British Army.

Walter became the first black Infantry Officer in the history
of the British Army. This was an amazing event as
the official Army law said that officers had to be of
"pure European descent" and Walter's father had come
from the Caribbean. Walter's strength of character and
his leadership talents meant that he was rewarded with
a promotion despite Army law. Walter was the first black
officer to take command of white soldiers and lead them
into battle, when it would have been very shocking to
some people, who still believed that black people were
inferior to white people.

Walter returned to France in August 1917 and rejoined the Middlesex Regiment, where he was given his first group of soldiers to command. There were some advantages to being an officer. Walter was given four meals a day instead of three, he was paid more and could take more leave. However, with these privileges came the responsibility of looking after his men. Walter used his experiences of playing professional football to make sure that his soldiers became part of a new team, one where the men looked out for each other when they were going into battle.

Coolness under fire

The first major battle that Walter Tull led his men into was known as Passchendaele, in June 1917. The village of Passchendaele in Belgium was built near marshland. The weather was so cold and wet and the area so swampy, that the land turned into a mud bath. Many soldiers and horses drowned when they fell into deep holes made by shells. Even tanks, developed during the First World War, were defeated by the mud.

Conditions for Walter and his men were very unpleasant: they were cold, wet, tired and bogged down by the mud. Despite months of fighting against the Germans, the **Allies** won very little ground.

When the battle ended, in November 1917, only five miles of land had been won and over 200,000 Allied soldiers had been killed, the equivalent to 5 centimetres for every soldier that died. Walter wrote to his brother Edward that the Germans were bombing the British trenches "like a demon" and that he was lucky to have escaped without any injuries. He described "dodging about from trench to trench" trying to find a safe passage away from the shells that were exploding all around him. "We were lucky and got to a tunnel which would help us on our way considerably. Unfortunately, the outlet was flooded and we got soaked up to our hips."

A spying mission

After surviving the battle of Passchendaele, the Middlesex Regiment was moved to northern Italy to fight against the Germans and the Austrians. Instead of fighting in trenches the soldiers often lived in the woods, with the River Piave flowing between the British and the Germans. Dangerous missions were undertaken to cross the river to spy on the enemy.

On Christmas Eve 1917, Walter led a small group of men on one of these missions. They had to cross a bridge over the River Piave in the middle of the night and spy on the Germans. Bridges over the Piave were under constant attack from enemy fire, so it was safer for Walter and his men to cross under the cover of darkness when it would be more difficult for the Germans to see them. Walter and his men completed their mission and returned with vital information about the enemy.

A few days later, on New Year's Eve, Walter again led his men across the fast-flowing River Piave, but this time their job was even more dangerous. They had to lead the attack against the enemy, capture any prisoners and hold their position so that another bridge could be built behind them. Walter used all the skills he'd learnt in his officer training to complete the mission successfully.

When he returned without losing a single man, Walter was praised by his commanding officer, Major General Sydney Lawford, for his "gallantry and coolness". Walter was recommended for a medal for officers known as the Military Cross for his bravery during the mission.

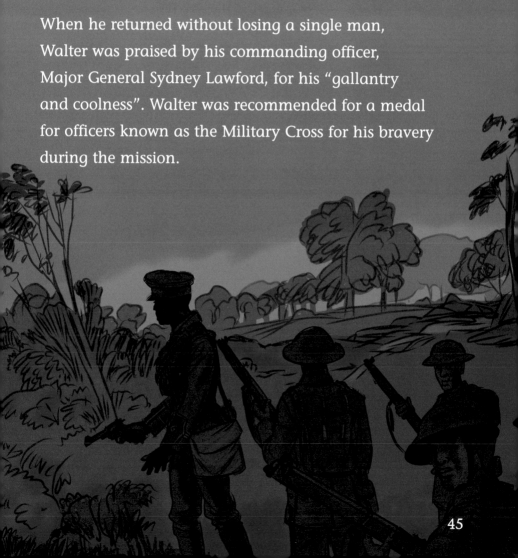

Death of a hero

After his success in northern Italy, Walter was transferred back to France. The British Army was preparing to defend itself from a major German attack and in March 1918 the second Battle of the Somme began. Walter and his men moved to a small town called Favreuil and waited for the attack. On the morning of 25 March, the Germans began to bomb the front line and launched their attack on the British trenches.

As Walter was commanding his men, a machine-gun bullet hit him through the back of his neck. He was killed instantly. Walter's friend, the Leicester goalkeeper, Private Billingham, made a heroic attempt to rescue Walter's body, but when he realised that his own life was too much at risk, he returned empty handed. Walter's body was left on the battlefield of the Somme.

On 17 April 1918 a **telegram** arrived at 419 St Vincent Street in Glasgow, the home of Edward Tull, informing him of Walter's death. The Tulls were a close and caring family, and Edward later told his daughter, Jean, that receiving the news of his brother's death was one of the worst moments of his life.

Edward learns of Walter's death.

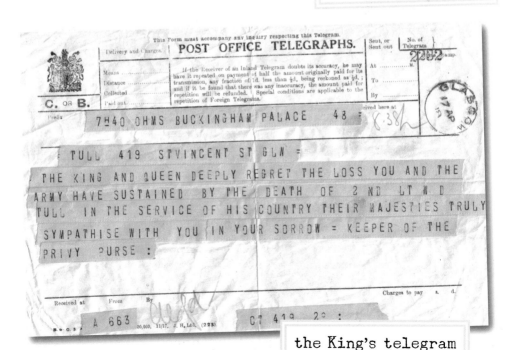

This Form must accompany any inquiry respecting this Telegram.

POST OFFICE TELEGRAPHS.

Sent, or Sent out | No. of Telegram

Delivery and Charges.

Means

Distance

Collected

Paid out

C. OR B.

If the Receiver of an Inland Telegram doubts its accuracy, he may have it repeated on payment of half the amount originally paid for its transmission, any fraction of 1d. less than ½d. being reckoned as ½d.; and if it be found that there was any inaccuracy, the amount paid for repetition will be refunded. Special conditions are applicable to the repetition of Foreign Telegrams.

At .... M.

To ....

By ....

ived here at

7H40 OHMS BUCKINGHAM PALACE   48 =   8·38

TULL   419   STVINCENT ST GLN =

THE KING AND QUEEN DEEPLY REGRET THE LOSS YOU AND THE ARMY HAVE SUSTAINED BY THE DEATH OF 2 ND LT W D TULL IN THE SERVICE OF HIS COUNTRY THEIR MAJESTIES TRULY SYMPATHISE WITH YOU IN YOUR SORROW = KEEPER OF THE PRIVY PURSE :

Charges to pay   s.   d.

Received at   From   By

A 663   00,000. 11/17. J. H.,Ltd. (223)   CT 419   2° :

the King's telegram

In a letter written to Edward in April 1918, Walter's Commanding Officer, Major Poole, wrote that Walter "was very cool in moments of danger and always volunteered for any enterprise that might be of service ... His courage was of a high order and was combined with a quiet and unassuming manner."

Walter Tull – from footballer to military hero

Remembering Walter Tull

At the end of the First World War, Walter's name was placed on the Arras Memorial, a few miles away from Favreuil where he was killed. The Memorial has the names of 35,000 soldiers from Britain, South Africa and New Zealand who have no grave. There are also 2,650 graves in the cemetery, including soldiers from the West Indies Regiment and the German Army.

Arras Memorial, France

Outside Northampton Town's football stadium, at the top of a road called Walter Tull Way, is a large stone memorial. On it are carved words that were written to remember Walter Tull, footballer, officer and hero.

Glossary

abolition	when a law or custom is ended
Allies	soldiers who fought for Britain, France and America
amateur	a sportsperson who plays for no money
auctions	where something is sold to the highest bidder
British Empire	a group of countries spanning the globe that were once ruled by Great Britain
contract	a legally binding agreement
debut	first appearance in a particular role
demoralised	loss of confidence or hope
enlist	to join the armed forces
First Division	the top division of the English Football League between 1888 and 1992
Infantry Officer	an officer in the British Army trained to fight on foot
initiative	being able to think and act independently
Lance Sergeant	an old officer rank in the British Army that was a third or fourth promotion
league	a group of football teams that play each other during a season for a championship
leave	time off
racist	someone who does not like people who are a different colour or race
slave	someone who is forced to work for another against their will
telegram	a message sent along wires by a machine called a telegraph, then printed out

Index

Walter Tull timeline

Walter is born
in Folkestone,
Kent

Walter becomes an
amateur footballer
for Clapton

Walter becomes
a professional
footballer for
Tottenham Hotspur

1888

1906

1909

1897

1908

1909

Walter and Edward
sent to the children's
home in London

Clapton wins the
Amateur Football
Championships

Walter goes on
tour with Tottenham
Hotspur to
South America

54

Walter becomes
an officer and
leads his men at
Passchendaele,
the first black man
to lead white soldiers
into battle

Walter transfers to
Northampton Town
Football Club

Walter is
promoted to
Lance Sergeant

1911

1915

1917

1914

Walter joins
the Army

1916

Walter fights in
his first major
battle, the Somme

1918

Walter is killed in
action at the second
Battle of the Somme

Ideas for guided reading

Learning objectives: understand underlying themes, causes and points of view; improvise using a range of drama strategies to explore hopes, fears and desires

Curriculum links: Citizenship: Living in a diverse world; History: How has life in Britain changed since 1948?

Interest words: abolition, allied soldiers, amateur, apprentice, auctions, battalion, British Empire, Colonel, contract, debut, enlist, First Division, grenade, Infantry Officer, initiative, Lance Sergeant, league, Lieutenant, plantation, prejudice, racist, regiment, slave, telegram

Resources: writing materials

Getting started

This book can be read over two or more guided reading sessions.

- Explain to the group that this is a biography. Discuss what a biography is and what purpose it serves, e.g. to show the life of an interesting or important person.

- Ask one of the children to read the blurb and as a group look at the cover image. Why do they think Walter Tull's life is considered to be important?

- Discuss the word *discrimination* and what children think this can relate to, e.g. age, colour, race, religion. Can they give any examples of prejudice from either their own lives, or those of others?

Reading and responding

- Encourage children to read independently to p29 and make notes of key moments in Walter's life in their own words, including their own opinion of events.

- As a group, discuss two questions: What qualities did Walter have which made him successful in the football field? What obstacles did he need to overcome? Encourage children to refer to the text in their answers, e.g. *Walter was loyal because he kept in close contact with his brother,* and *Prejudice was an obstacle in his game against Bristol.*